# Eric Bloodaxe?

## AND OTHER VERSE

Copyright © Phil Poyser 2014
*All rights reserved*

The right of Phil Poyser to be identified as the author
of this work has been asserted by him in accordance with
the Berne Convention.

First published in Great Britain in 2014 by
Phil Poyser Publications.

ISBN-13: 978-1500925727

ISBN-10: 1500925721

All rights reserved. No part of this publication may be reproduced,
stored in a retrieval system, or transmitted, in any form or by any means,
electronic, mechanical, photocopying, recording or otherwise,
without the prior permission of the publisher or copyright owner.

Cover Copyright © Karen Ross 2014

http://www.krossart.co.uk

## Contents

| | |
|---|---|
| Eric Bloodaxe? | Page Five |
| Jodrell Bank | Page Six |
| Bad VB-rations | Page Six |
| Hot Tea/Cold Age | Page Seven |
| Breakfast Table | Page Eight |
| Rock and Roll | Page Nine |
| Canals | Page Ten |
| Moonstuck | Page Eleven |
| No Sex Please We're British | Page Twelve |
| On the Shoulders of Giant Gums | Page Thirteen |
| The Coat | Page Fourteen |
| London Omnibus | Page Fifteen |
| Disorganised Crime | Page Sixteen |
| No Title After all these Years | Page Sixteen |
| Allotment Year | Page Seventeen |
| Wistful Twister | Page Eighteen |
| Jason and the Come-to-Noughts | Page Nineteen |
| Yellow Car | Page Twenty-One |
| Captain Ahab | Page Twenty-Three |
| Man and Superman | Page Twenty-Four |
| Uranus 1781 | Page Twenty-Five |
| Haiku 34: Chompionship | Page Twenty-Five |
| Blood on the Tracks | Page Twenty-Six |
| Seascape with Gulls | Page Twenty-Seven |
| Cricket Bat Calypso | Page Twenty-Eight |
| The Proof Readers Valentine | Page Twenty-Nine |
| The Space | Page Thirty |

To Mady
who puts up
with an awful lot,
this is for you.

Also in memory of
Andrew Grant,
friend, scientist, running mate
and football fan, who
died 29/12/2012, aged 49.

# Eric Bloodaxe?

He was quiet and introverted. A nod would just suffice.
He minded his own business, wouldn't pry at any price.
He nurtured his allotment plot with tender loving care,
but sometimes you might catch him with a far off, wistful stare.

He'd sit down with his mug of tea, well-earned mid-morning break,
or pause from planting labours and lean hard upon his rake.
His head would fill with images that frankly he deplored.
He had no explanation as shrill noises howled and roared.

It seemed he manned a long boat oar with rough and calloused hands.
He'd crossed the sea at risk of life to reach these hostile lands.
He wore a Viking helmet, by his side his trusty axe,
which hung there at the ready till he reached their squalid shacks.

Blood-curdling oaths he'd utter as he lashed out left and right.
 He never gave a second thought, just hacked with all his might
and speed was of the essence ere the men folk would return:
seize what they could, then back to sea and leave the huts to burn.

Were Eric's ancestral voices an echo from his genes?
He mulled this concept over as he hoed his peas and beans.
These days he rakes and tillages. It's spuds that he will sack
and only in odd moments DNA will draw him back.

The distant past lies buried and long gone those roving bands.
Nowadays, blood, fish and bone meal, it is on Eric's hands.
So, pass the time of day with him, then leave him to his work.
For there's the faintest, outside chance that Eric'll go berserk.

## Jodrell Bank : A Rhyme Against Humanity

Permanently eavesdropping on the teeming emptiness of space,
Jodrell Bank's our local, hand-cupped earpiece of the human race.
It listens out for cosmic contact for which we've always yearned,
a moment touched with trepidation out of fear of being spurned;
the wonder and the horror when it dawns we aren't unique,
that Earth is not the one-off, one-trick, Universe's freak.
For there is no way of knowing what might be taken as the norm:
they might be the same as we are ... or an intelligent life form!


## Bad VB-rations

My name it is Victoria. I've loads and loads of dosh.
I also have a hubby and we're known as Becks and Posh.
Now I'm the one who's famous, He was just a Man U. hero,
but I was once THE Spice Girl before I was size zero.
I'm bringing back this pair of jeans disgusted that they've shrunk.
How dare you! Me, put on weight? I eat like a Buddist monk.
You'll never sell another pair. I'll make sure of that.
You'll pay for implying I might have an ounce of fat.
What's that I hear you mutter? I should go and see a shrink.
If my lashes weren't so heavy, you'd see me pout and blink.
I'm off to an emporium where they know a girl with taste
and buy an outfit fits so tight, it helps keep David chaste.

# Hot Tea / Cold Age

Thanks for dropping in to see me.
I love to chat and have a cup of tea.
There's nothing like a proper brew
with milk and sugar. Just between us two,
the doctor kicks up such a fuss
and nags so. He's such a sourpuss,
makes me do those aerobatics.
Well, they just don't understand rheumatics
and pills don't take the pain away ……
You know, I've had a really lovely day.

It's a while now since you called by ?
I think you must have something in your eye.
There's nothing beats a piping cuppa
to get you from breakfast through to supper.
They make it with my favourite brand.
At least that's what I'm led to understand.
I'll always drink a second cup,
especially if my bronnie's playing up.
You came by only yesterday ? ……
I've had, I'm sure I've had, a lovely day.

And such a pretty bunch of flowers
and heady scent, so strong it overpowers.
Should I try another biscuit ?
Rich Tea ? Do you think that I should risk it ?
I wonder why my Dad's not been ?
I said so to ……… You know the one I mean,
the lady who ….. Now what's her name ?
Dear oh dear. Still I'm very glad you came …..
They'll come to take away the tray ……
I've had, I'm almost sure, a lovely day.

I draw a breath or two and pause,
then cross the room to join this world of yours.

Each time you greet me from your chair.
We sit and talk. You go on, unaware.
Go through the same exchanges,
sit so close and yet we could be strangers,
you, in your private world, marooned
in Time, with shadows, ghosts, the dead, cocooned ……
but in a funny kind of way,
dear Mum, you always have a lovely day.

## Breakfast Table

Imagine a mangrove tree, uprooted and transplanted:
four stout trunks thrust upwards,
merging tongue and groove
into a platform, a flat form,
on which, in some strange symmetry,
and not unlike the acorns on an oak,
the egg cups, with their brown-shelled fruit, grow.

# Rock and Roll
## or Between a Rock and a Hard Disc

The rock missed its mark by a "hare's breath"
and the rabbit, chastened but unharmed,
bounded away, white tail warning signal
hoisted.
And that should really have been that ......

but the rock was unusually smooth and round,
a form teased out over many years
by the harsh caress of nearby glacial streams.
It had fitted snugly into the hunter's hand.

Now, tonight's hunger pangs still far off,
his eyes followed the missile's path
as it rolled and bounced, unhindered,
down the slope, until it came to rest many strides away.

At one point it disturbed another stone
and the pair revolved, briefly side by side,
then in tandem, finally, separately,
to settle where destiny dictated.

Somewhere deep in his subconscious,
the hunter felt a strange, warm glow.
The picture of the smooth rotation
linked itself to other pressing images
that the daily struggle for survival presented.

He loped to where his weapon lay,
retrieved the rock and let it drop again.
Round and round, down and down it went.
Surprised by his own delight,
a childish cry escaped: "Whee!"

Gathered round the fire that night,

sharing the frugal provision of fellow hunters,
more skilful stalkers with straighter aim,
he conveyed by stick and dirt
the picture in his mind: the rock,
the slope, the rotation, the excitement.
"Whee! Whee!", he repeated.
"Wheel?" came the puzzled retort. "Wheel?"

## Canals

Canals may no longer be the life blood,
the arteries of industrial heart- and hinterland.
Some may be clogged with rushes, silt and mud.
Some bear famous names: Grand Union or simply Grand,
"where Doges wed the sea with rings" (in quotes).
Gondolas? Browning, give me our narrow boats!

From first sod cut, 5 years in the completion,
a marathon in length from end to end,
it may not stand comparisons Venetian,
but Macclesfield's canal, content to wend
from Marple south through a dozen Bosley locks,
by ancient mills, passed fields of grazing flocks,

unassuming, slinks far beneath Mow Cop
to join the Trent and Mersey at Hall Green.
It's residence to squabbling ducks which flop
and home to boats with names like "Faerie Queen",
some nomadic, some on permanent moorings
and victims of some poet's daft outpourings.

The patient fishermen seem cast in stone
till early morning joggers plod too near.
Dog walker ambles by with mobile phone.
His mutt, stick clenched in mouth, not clutched to ear,
disturbs a gawky heron at its task.
Peace, beauty, freely shared: what more is there to ask?

# Moonstuck: Neil Armstrong (1930-2012)

Hey, diddle, diddle.
It's a bit of a riddle.
Neil Armstrong, who walked on the moon,
and Buzz Aldrin laughed once they had done
and their module was docked again soon.

Then back down on earth, Neil questioned the worth
of his fame and the toll it would take.
He was wanted by all and was always on call,
an appetite he couldn't slake.

He was dined and fêted. It never abated.
He was the toast, the talk of the town..
This man of few words said, "Fame is absurd.
It's a burden I want to put down".

Once from NASA resigned, he had peace of mind,
he settled on a farm in Ohio.
Over vast fields of maize, he would steadfastly gaze
at the stars and the moon in the sky, oh.

And he knew he had been and the earth was blue-green
by the light of the moon bright and shiny.
"What more to achieve?" he would quietly grieve,
"We are dust specks that breathe. We are tiny."

At age 82, his time here was through
and he passed into History's charge.
It was time to find peace, all his atoms release
and his fame and his name are writ large.

# No Sex, Please, We're British

Whilst the French have the can can and Follies Bergères,
a delight when one's feeling skittish.
On this side the channel we avoid flesh that's bare.
We're known for "No Sex, Please, We're British".

But is this the British Isles' real state of affairs?
Can this be the State of our Nation?
Is the fault Cameron-Clegg's or just Brown and Blair's?
Surely populace needs copulation.

Now the Irish divide into Catholics or Prods
and a good Catholic genuflects.
He won't wear a condom. It's abhorred by his gods.
Father Jack's only comments were "fecks".

And what of the Scotsman, our far northern cousin?
We wouldn't be showing our respects
if we didn't mention when he wants half a dozen,
Wee Willie will just growl, "Gi' me sex".

And of course when you're staying north of the border
and in whisky stills up to the hilt,
a Scotsman will tell you all's in working order
for nothing is worn under his kilt.

And in "Under Milk Wood", there are strange goings on:
it's night time and everyone's dreaming.
Often it's sex the sleepers are dwelling upon.
It's llewd, llustful, llurid and steaming.

So we're left with the English and stiff upper lips,
though an aspect one sometimes neglects
is a stiffening somewhere near pelvis and hips.
Gosh, the English are normal at sex.

# On The Shoulders of Giant Gums

The philosopher mathematician, Isaac Newton,
would often sit beneath an apple tree with fruit on
and on theorems, laws and other res mathematical
reflect on working days and even days sabbatical
and thus with knotty points the polymath would grapple
with gravitas, until the time there fell an apple.

"This earth-bound fruit is falling with a force of 1 g,"
surmised the sage, "which will apply to jump of bungee.
This shall surely come to pass or my name's not Isaac."
Futuristic vision or just another wisecrack ?
"Were I in Spain, I'd sleep 'neath fragrant orange tree,
thus navel contemplating whilst letting thoughts roam free.

In Canada, I would muse under the lonesome pine,
watch cones, not apples, dropping, as in the Grand Design.
but had I lain 'neath giant gum in Terr' Australis,
methinks I would have seen the aurora polaris,
suffered fatal outcome from a cranial cavity
and let someone else expound the Law of Gravity."

For underneath the shoulders of mighty giant gums
is not a place to seek the shade, nor to do one's sums.
Deep in the forests of the 60 metre tingle,
where eucalypts of every kind profusely mingle,
it might be said, although with a certain levity,
it could ne'er be known as Newton's Law of "Grevity".

# The Coat.

The morning sun was tempered by a breeze on Beachy Head.
The seagulls wheeled and hovered and complained they were unfed.
Our hands thrust deep in pockets and our faces to the wind,
we talked of times now long since gone and joked and wryly grinned.

Across the grass just touched by Spring, we climbed towards the top
and gingerly, with thumping hearts, we peeked into the drop.
The grey waves lashed the pebbled strand the length of Beachy Head.
Someone had jumped without a word. They'd left their coat instead.

Had they felt like they were flying as they fell towards the sea?
That weakest force, earth's gravity, it was would set them free.
It's a second. It's eternity. Mixed despair and thrill?
Did it provide the answer when they'd finally had their fill?

The patient sea so slowly gnaws away at Beachy Head,
whilst human mayflies flit their hour and pass from live to dead.
A crumpled, cast-off coat is like that body in the sea.
We thought about our fellow man. We thought of you and me.

A whisky bottle briefly bobs, then sinks without a trace
and Beachy Head's the journey from the cliff top to its base.
Salt water brings a silence once it's poured into the throat.
The wind is left to whisper soft and sigh: "I'll get me coat".

# London Omnibus: A Flashback
## or Poetry in Motion

Omnibus ………….
Now there's a word packed full of meaning
or passengers of course, if you take mine;
the double-decker ………
not without its ambiguities ………
the colour of Flanders' pillar boxes,
swanning along Kensington High Street,
stuttering along the Strand
or via Clapham Junction
or edging along the King's Road
in those heady, whirlwind Sixties,
swinging in the rain,
mini-skirted dolly bird,
handbag bouncing on its lead,
over her shoulder (goes one care),
and my appreciative eyes
lifted towards heaven,
following her progress
up the stairs to Smokers' Paradise.

Post-Scriptum:-

And now, of course, we're in our Sixties.
Let's hope we've both grown old disgracefully,
ignored the pull of gravity and gravitas
thrown caution, dulce and decorum to the whirlwind,
handbagged and bounced our way through Life.
Who ever you are, wherever you are, you're here,
always carefree, always making your hay upstairs
in the omnibus edition:

and from mini-flirt to maxi-ISA,
we're still young inside and no damned wiser.

## Disorganised Crime

It was anagram time for Al Capone
and the F.I.B. agents were closing in.
"I've-'a no place' to run" he cried,
taxing their patience to the max.

"Merci", begged the Mafioso,
looking slightly crossword puzzled.
That's disorganised crime for you
and, coincidentally, the answer to 1 down (5).

## No Title After All These Years

In the intimacy of the darkness,
entwined, we lose ourselves.
Surfacing, we gasp for air, with eyes tight shut
against the glaring brightness of our self-revelation.
(Such poor blind eyes they are).
And the ears, deafened by the roaring silence,
make the mute tongue wag.

There is a foretaste of mortality
in the very act of procreation.
There is an ancestral smell
just beyond the limits of detection.
There is, on the skin, the tangible rime of history.

The senses, dulled, confused,
shiver at the loneliness
of one man in the echoing universe
of a woman's arms.

# Allotment Year

As wisps of night evaporate and teetering gate posts lurch,
upon the highest greenhouse roof, the blackbird claims his perch.
Another early bird's arrived and startled pigeons flap.
A gardener's here to plant his crops before mid-morning nap.

He's done his preparation and replenished tired soil,
Manure and compost double dug will soon reward his toil.
Desultory prods with trowels made, it's time to have a brew
and sit and sip and sip and sit and watch the shoots break through.

Returning sun has warmed the ground. Some rocket's gone to seed
Inspection day will soon be round. He clears his plot of weed,
but almost as he watches, they're thrusting up again.
He scores the same as last year, only seven out of ten.

There are subtle, precious pleasures that come with Grow-Your-Own:
there's how to judge the seasons; there's how to spell home "groan";
there's the taste of new potatoes freshly lifted from the ground;
and he's no need of sun-bed hire, he's organically browned.

Then once a year, he has the chance to show in head-to-head
the produce of his gardening skills from each and every bed,
and, not at all contrary, prove how cherished gardens grow
and chant that age old mantra: "Dig, plant, pick your crops and go".

# Wistful Twister or I Should Be So Lucky

"Of all crazy games that were ever in vogue,
I'd love to play "Twister" with Kylie Minogue,
though on reflection, it would still be for nought.
Like basketball, Twister's a non-contact sport."

"With bodies contorted (I'd bend mine like Becks,
and stifle all thoughts of the opposite sex)
and mind concentrating on neutral gender,
I'd lean over backwards so as not to offend her."

"Stop there before it gets any sillier.
You're too old for acute Kyliephilia."
"Don't be a drongo," I mutter quite shyly,
"How else would I live my dreamtime with Kylie ?"

"For it's not in, it's uncool, it's not à la mode.
A game of society alone is plain odd.
The question arises : Why's Life so unfair
and I end up playing "Twister" solitaire ?"

# Jason and the Come-to-Noughts

Yo, man! Eh, we 'ad a right laugh on Sat'day night,
off our faces and aht of it.
We was hangin' out with Ryan. He's alright,
and his girl, Jade, well, she's real fit.

This crap car was like parked on the pavement,
so Liam he gives it a kick.
Trace, she's gob-smacked and screams in amazement:
"What yer doin', yer stupid dick?"

Now our Jason, he's been doin' Thai kickin'
and the mirrah's right in his way.
While Courtney sees if there's owt there worth nickin',
he Bruce Lee's it like it's a gay.

There's a crack and the bits are scatt'rin' all over.
The mirrah goes fuckin' flyin'
and shatters like one of them star super nova.
This nosey old git he starts spyin'.

I can see him peerin' and chunterrin' away.
Then he's on the 'phone in a flash.
and he's shoutin', "You bloody vandals'll pay!",
all posh with a military 'tash'.

Leg it? No way. We're 'ard and we don't give a fuck
for any old bastard or t'cops.
So, we walks away cool and finger the schmuck.
Then out of this cop car there 'ops

a uniformed kid not that much older than you.
There are ten of us, one of him. Yo!
"Right, you lot, listen up. I've got a question or two".
He glances round at the bimbo

who looks a bit like, is it Cagney or Lacey?,
calling all cars on this phone thing.
Some of the lads are shitting their pants. So's Tracey.
I says, "What's up? We've done nuffing."

He points at me and says like, "Don't come the hothead.
When I want you to speak, you'll know.
Who broke that mirror? You know you were spotted.
Own up and the others can go."

They must think that there's like one born every minute.
We just stared him right in the eyes.
We knew there was no way they could hope to pin it
on Jason or none of us guys.

Just then, three cars and police motorbikes various
drew up like the Bill do on tele'.
It was getting too heavy, too fuckin' serious.
I'd loved to have giv'n them some welly.

We let them rant on and try to intimidate.
We looked at the floor not to grin.
They went on till my nerves were starting to grate.
I needed a handy sick bin.

"It were only like a fuckin' mirrah, Sarge" I said.
"Aye, a mirror on society",
he shoots back. What's that bleedin' well about? Dickhead.
I can't stand their bleedin'-heart piety.

# Yellow Car

The car was certainly yellow.
The rest is a bit of a blur.
I was the wrong side of mellow.
My speech was beginning to slur.

I'd been out too long on the razz
(Well, I'm sure you know how it is).
I made a mistake. Everyone has.
It's mad to mix spirits and fizz.

I went to cross, no denying,
and before I knew what was what,
I was up in the air. I went flying.
A wise thing to do, it was not.

The world went into slow motion.
I bounced once or twice, yet was calm.
Of the outcome, I hadn't a notion.
Could I hear the 23rd. Psalm?

The Lord is my Shepherd? Am I flock?
I hadn't been drinking still water,
so must have been suffering shock
and feared that my life would be shorter.

The driver jumped out, pale and shaken.
She asked, "Are you OK?" and stooped.
The drink it was saved my bacon.
I was bruised and my ego had drooped.

I was stunned, but she was more stunning,
the sunset entwined in her hair.
I summoned my animal cunning
and winced. She said, "Does it hurt? Where?"

"Can you walk? You must seek attention.
It's not far to Macc's A and E".
From me, there was no dissension.
I was head over heels, you see,

The long wait passed in a blinking.
The mind plays some curious tricks.
"One over the eight", you are thinking.
After all, she had knocked me for six.

It turned out that we both were musicians,
struck a chord. There was real empathy
and whilst we awaited physicians
A and E echoed to our R and B.

The car is certainly yellow.
It's parked out in front. Can you see?
I play the drums, she plays cello,
then we cuddle and play our CD.

I hope it will always be yellow,
Whatever the tint, shade or hue
and whether on foot or on velo',
I'll still be knocked over by Sue.

# Captain Ahab: The Real Story

They call me "Captain" Ahab, though I've never been to sea.
My story's been narrated in Melville's biography.
Whilst some of it is truthful, there's a twist within this tale.
He writes about old Moby Dick, the murd'rous "Great White Whale".

Many qualities had Hermann, but he had two tiny faults:
rather hard of hearing and over fondness for the malts.
When to him my quest described, my obsessive Holy Grail,
I'd said to him, "To hell I'd go to catch "The Great White Quail"".

I'm here to clear my conscience and to set the records straight.
I'll no longer feel the need Hermann Melville to berate.
'Twas in the Scottish Highlands. We were never under sail.
You can ask either of our beaters, Queequeg or Ishmael.

There were never any harpoons. "The Pequod" was a cart.
Our lives were not in danger. I've my hand upon my heart,
but through the bogs and heather, we were hot upon the trail
of the one and only Moby Dick, fearsome Great White Quail.

He'd often come upon us from the side we'd least expect
It didn't seem to help however many times we'd checked.
The struggle, long and gruesome, he would fight us tooth and nail
and any day I'd rather face a hundred like that whale.

He'd come at us with his claws out and with his beak he pecked.
We would have been right foolish not to treat him with respect.
But once we'd up and bagged him, there's no blubber of the whale
could ever hope to rival that of sweetest pan-fried quail.

# Man and Superman

My disguise is quite authentic:
dull, late 60s, humanoid.
My persona is eccentric.
My poems often nod to Freud.

But just beneath this outer coat
of liberal, middle-brower,
there lurks a crime-wave antidote,
a superpowered ker-pow-er.

When devastation's on the cards,
when Macclesfield Town's attacked,
when councils lift the last safeguards
and short-sighted plans are backed,

I don my underpants and cloak
in some quiet deserted spot
and suddenly I'm Superbloke,
so don't mess with me. Best not.

Developers' mad plans are dropped
and the council soon recants.
My alter ego I adopt
when I wear my underpants.

Clad in lycra®, cloak and undies,
small town villains fear my name.
I'll work weekdays, Sat'days, Sundays.
No job's too wild nor too tame.

I've been known to swoop on bullies
or when litter vandals strike
and drop rubbish in our gullies,
Superbloke's back on his bike.

So, remember when a crisis
needs resolving at a stroke,
I'll perform my next ecdysis
and emerge as Superbloke.


## Uranus : 1781

Sir William Herschel, known as "Willie",
stared into deepest space until he
upon a distant planet chanced.
Around his telescope he danced.

"I am the first that has ever seen
this planet. If only we'd a queen
I'd name it after her. Our King
is "George" and t'were a pretty thing!

To use the royal name would gain us
ignominy. And so "Uranus"
is my choice. Take good care how stressed.
On its first syllable is best.


## Haiku 34 : The Chompionship

Twinkle toes and teeth,
Luis Suárez, Uruguay's
inter-gnasher-nal.

# Blood on the Tracks

I've been to Chorlton-cum-Hardy.
I've been to Nelson in Lancs.
I've been to Trafalgar, the Cape and the Square,
but never saw blood on the planks.

I've been to Boothtown and Lincoln.
I've been to the Ford on the Ox.
I've been to both Washingtons, that's ours and theirs,
but never saw blood in the box.

I've been to the Twistle of Oswald
and to Chorley's Camelot Palace.
I've passed through Kennedy City, MN.
but never saw blood run in Dallas.

I've been to towns called Dakota.
and to Chapman Uni, CA.
I've flown from John Lennon airport.
but blood didn't go flying that day.

I've been to Mexico city
to a suburb called Coyoacán.
I've been to Aldema Mercader and Léon
but that's not where Trotsky's blood ran.

I've been to Mount Calvary, Wisconsin.
I've been to Nazareth town.
I've seen the Dead sea and far Galilee,
but that's not where they took Jesus down.

The stories you read in the Gospels
may not be all based on hard facts,
but you can't deny the effect that they've had:
holy wars have left blood on the tracts.

It's wrong to have sex for enjoyment.
You can't use a condom for AIDS
to be safe from blood and bodily fluids,
but I still harp on back to Crusades.

For now we have the jihadists
who'll readily die for their cause.
They'll blow themselves up, not just self-destruct.
And the blood that spills? Theirs, mine and yours.

## Seascape with Gulls

This is too good to last.
It must be just that moment in the seagull day
when the unfortunate silver-scaled sild
has given up the ghost in the digestive juices,
succumbed to its fate, stopped swimming against the tide
and started that strange metamorphosis
on its final journey from sardine to gull.
The hosts meanwhile feel an all-pervading, dull contentment.
Not such a bad old world after all.

Any moment now, this herring gull symmetry
will be shattered as, first one,
(in all probability, the one nearest my vantage point)
will shift its weight uneasily from one leg to the other,
glance nervously round at nothing in particular,
emit that raucous screech of alarm or disdain
or "F… you, Jimmy" or "Bandits at 3 o'clock",
and, with the coolest stretch of its wings,
fall upwards into the wind,
to be followed, in perfect formation
by the whole squadron, peeling off like Spitfires,
into the wild, grey yonder.

# Cricket Bat Calypso

My bat is in pristine condition,
though it isn't much younger than me.
If I were an artist like Titian,
I would paint it for posterity.

O cricket bat, my cricket bat,
for smackin' ball, not swattin' gnat.
O cricket bat, my cricket bat,
stroke it through the covers. Howzat?

We'd gone to the Notts. match at Steetley,
had my mammy and pappy and me.
The pros hit the ball oh so sweetly,
they'd reached more than 300 by tea.

O cricket bat, my cricket bat,
for smackin' ball, not swattin' gnat.
O cricket bat, my cricket bat,
pull it through mid-wicket. Howzat?

This was Cyril Poole's benefit season,
the raffle prize an autographed bat.
We all used to love it when he's in,
so we bought us some tickets for that.

O cricket bat, my cricket bat,
for smackin' ball, not swattin' gnat.
O cricket bat, my cricket bat,
leg glance it to the boundary. Howzat?

In the raffle my ticket was drawn out,
so that autographed bat it was mine.
Mammy she scream and pappy he shout
and Old Man Sun he started to shine.

O cricket bat, my cricket bat,
for smackin' ball, not swattin' gnat.
O cricket bat, my cricket bat,
late cut it through the gulley. Howzat?

On the bat: four counties; two nations;
retired, they drink sun-downers with ice.
Some still watch the next generations
and some wear their whites in Paradise.

O cricket bat, my cricket bat,
for smackin' ball, not swattin' gnat.
O cricket bat, my cricket bat,
Straight drive it for a big 6. Howzat?

## The Proof Reader's Valentine

To write these words, I've opted for
a script they call Times New Romance.
The fond size is adopted more
by luck, good fortune, happenstance.

12 point seems right (size 12 to you).
Please say you'd hate it bigger.
I'm asking you to be my Roo.
I'll be your bouncy Tigger.

**I trust that this is not too bold**
*and your thought's not "smart italic",*
for that which glisters may be gold
though for men it's often phallic.

<u>So let me underline my plan</u>:
I will be yours if you are mine.
Forget the lines which do not scan,
my first edition Valentine.

# The Space (Just Above The Urinal)

Just above the urinal,
where the adverts for prostate hypertrophy
and Viagra usually fill the field of vision
and catch the vacant stare of those seeking relief,
giving rise to that universal downward glance of doubt
at the double edged sword of middle-aged manhood,
the yellowing plaster nursed a forehead-shaped dint.

The oval periphery of the crater had crumpled,
uncovering the coarse pink plaster grains,
but the centre was somehow through to bare brick.
This had been a sudden collision, followed by prolonged contact.
Either this man had been seriously pissed
or there had been an unreported, high magnitude earthquake
in the vicinity of Nottingham,
possibly due to subsidence from all those closed pits.

The forensic scientist might extrapolate thus:
"Male, around 1 metre 80 tall, heavily built,
blood alcohol levels in the region of 0.2%,
dangerously high and the result of consumption
of at least 12 units of alcohol
over a short period, say 3 hours.
DNA test markers from hair and skin fragments
reveal the man to be of late middle age and
from the North Notts. area, possibly Mansfield."

A police spokesman might say:
"The public are warned to stay away from this man.
He may be aggressive and easily provoked.
Do not look at him or his girlfriend.
He may take this as an affront
and an excuse to assault you and cause an affray.
Alternatively he may attempt to put his arm round you,

kiss you on the mouth and tell you
that you're a smashing bloke
and that he really, really loves you.
In either case, do not panic.
Ring 999 for assistance."

Place: "The Earl Of Chesterfield", on an insignificant, blue green planet near a small star in the Milky Way.
Time: early 21st. century, late evening and shortly before imminent catastrophic climate change.
"Last Orders, gentlemen, please".

Phil Poyser (seen reaching for his trusty quill) has been writing poetry (and the odd saga) for much longer than he can remember (1). Björn in 1944 in the Nottinghamshire mining village of Mansfield Woodhouse and encouraged by parents, Lucy and Vernon, to read, write and especially travel widely, he quickly took to using Norsey words until they had a quiet one with him (2). Educated (3) at Brunts Grammar school and Imperial College of Science and Technology (London), he rediscovered his love of Chemistry by setting off in 1966 on a voyage of (self)-discovery overland to Australia. He worked (4) at the Universidad de Concepción, Chile, the Université Louis Pasteur de Strasbourg and for ICI Pharma, Reims, France, and finally for ICI at Alderley Park, Cheshire, as it metamorphosed around him into Zeneca Pharmaceuticals and AstraZeneca. He's now a Food4Macc organic gardener, lives with his long-suffering partner, Mady, in Macclesfield, has two children, Paula and Michael, two step-children, Estelle and Hugo, two grandchildren, Samuel and Maxim and a grandkitten, Tibo. In his wilder moments, he thinks of himself as a kind of Doggerel Banksy.

(1) Editor: not really that long then. (2) Editor: yes, he's deaf. (3) Editor: you can't tell. (4) Editor: they couldn't tell.

Printed in Great Britain
by Amazon